# HURRY HOME HONEY

BY THE SAME AUTHOR:

*So we have been given time  Or* (Verse Press [now Wave Press], 2004)
*Nothing fictional but the accuracy or arrangement (she* (Quale Press, 2005)
*Texture Notes* (Letter Machine, forthcoming 2009)
    Translations:
*Four from Japan* (Litmus Press/Belladonna Books, 2006)
*To the Vast Blooming Sky* by Chika Sagawa (Seeing Eye Books, 2007)
*For the Fighting Spirit of the Walnut* by Takashi Hiraide (New Directions, 2008)

Sawako Nakayasu

# HURRY HOME HONEY

*Love Poems 1994-2004*

Burning Deck / Anyart, Providence

*Acknowledgments:*
Warm thanks to the editors that published these poems in the magazines *Key Satch(el)*, *Interlope, HOW2, Kenning, Poets & Poems, Upstairs at Duroc, New American Writing, 26, Cy Press, Chase Park, Antennae, Traverse, The Canary, Coconut, Ping•Pong, Conundrum, MiPOesias, Tinfish, Bombay Gin, Sous Rature*, and as chapbooks: *Balconic* (Duration Press e-chapbook), and *Clutch* (Tinfish Press).

"New Border Collapsing" has been included in the anthology *Stranger at Home: American Poetry with an Accent* (ed. Andrey Gritsman, Roger Weingarten, Kurt Brown, Carmen Firan), and performed improvisationally with Adachi Tomomi in *Movable Text* (Tokyo, 2003), and with Carl Stone at Café Metropol (Los Angeles, 2008).

"Glass" was digitally animated for live projection by the author, then performed with Yuli Hsu as part of *Wet Concrete Poetry* (Providence, 2001) and screened at the Dance & Media show (Tokyo, 2003). "Ice Event" was staged in San Diego as part of the show, *Tending the Keep.*

Thanks to Shigeru Kobayashi, Vermont Studio Center, Brown University, Africa Wayne, Miranda Yao, and Eugene Kang for helping to provide living and working space; to the Providence Lady Reds, Senior C Team, Silver Bullets, Rhodie Oldies, Puckheads, TSHA, Gino, Bubba, Mark, Chris, and everyone else in San Diego for the hockey; to John Granger, Carla Harryman, Joel Kuszai, Cole Heinowitz, Patrick Durgin, Mark Tardi, Forrest Gander, C.D. Wright, Don Kish, Chris Martin, Marianne Boruch, Kerri Sonnenberg, Jeffrey Weeter, Sally Picciotto, Laura Wright, Aaron Kunin, Steve Dolph, Jen Hofer, Anne Waldman and Joshua Edwards for insight, encouragement, and inspiration — with a special shout-out to Craig Watson, and Keith and Rosmarie Waldrop; to my family and to Eugene, for being there in the best ways possible.

Burning Deck is the literature program of Anyart: Contemporary Arts Center, a tax-exempt (501c3), non-profit organization.

Cover by Keith Waldrop

ISBN13: 978-1-886224-98-8, original paperback

*for the lovers and beloveds,*
*the almost loved, also loved, always loved*
*— and for eugene*

# CONTENTS

# I.

# BALCONIC

having been given corn*
having been given open*
                         a first time
having been given charge*
having been given heat*
having been given end*
                         an end
having been given frost, sweet, slip*
having been given charm*
having been given please*
having been given arms*
having been given boundary*
having been given call*
                         a rush
                         answer
having been given a line
having been given limbs
having been given distance
having been given conflict*
having been given all*
having been given bridge*
                         transport
having been given order*

having been given balcony
having been given balcony.

## The new predicament

states that no one is exempt. If you wake up on one side, you must. If you wake up on the other, again, there is no one to trust but. If you wake up and roll over, bump into a woman, all the more so. There is no bribe large enough, no drink strong enough to overcome the waves of people who will be waiting outside when you open your second-story balcony window. They may cheer, but more likely they will throw corn. Oh, they will throw corn. You will turn to your wife if you have one. She will rub her eyes. She will not say a thing, but the corn will come flying through the window. You will try hard not to look embarrassed. It will fly in silently.

What if she is hit by an ear?

## To give balcony

one would have it as a giving over of place, cover runs off
and towards, one would have it under such conditional
tense loaded moments as if one might bleed and bleed so
effortlessly, or bleed internally into its given corridors, as
if an everyday activity. To give balcony to a specified give
of body includes unclothing everything first and then time
and such will tell which parts, given with edges or good
will or given with all good edginess yet hopefulness.
Which parts which way. Yet the place remains where she
gives over for the first time, sex or surgery, at a time or all
over time, in a give of effort, increasingly, touching up,
and at both instances remaining what the fact.

## Before the hand furthers

*May I give you a power strip?*

The light in the palm waned yesterday. She worries, by necessity because this may lead to an outing for all. Even so, she persists in distributing bulbs to the needy, charges to the mothers. (Sometimes, on a whimsy, paint for nails.) The partner acts as glove, regarding warmth, support, sweat. The partner when under construction. Sometimes she wishes to talk extremities, in which case she is wrong most of the time, except for when she slaps a stray partner back into place: this she does with emollient grace, and grows her nails out later that very afternoon.

## Night looks down on me

while I write poems about the wrong balcony, try to store
them in the wrong parts of my body quaking, to fend off
the heat that you are not brewing for me inside as of
course you wouldn't or couldn't, being *in* the wrong *side*
and all moon ignored is better than acknowledged now,
mid-breath, while I withdraw my fingers full of no
point! no point! but my nails don't hold anyone up at all
and now look what I've written.

No wonder the night.

# Dead wedding b-

comes an altar to define to proceed to exteriorate to
parallel in white to curtain to black to esteem or to
estimate to accumulate to debt to overhang to celebriate
to pacifically witness to inundate to forecast away to
drain the red to parade to gentle tirade to simplifade to
run still to gaze to gauze to veil to fold to sign to look
out, over, beyon, to finalize

to close the d

## Disney wedding on the balcony

is made of (petrified) cake.
The broom gets up to dance
but the guests have all brided down below

So he sighs, heaves,
so he hoists her up above:

One,
two,
like tree
      She —
      felled overboard
spreads frosting all over the palace

The guests dive fro and fro —
"Too young,"
   shaking their head

## Frictionless on

the ball, mouth full of peas she steps out
she steps out
steps     of the cow palace
to your left,
                shoulder rearing up
right, larger than appearances
later than a youthful nocturnal a
                    chug full of light

to the clean rinse & dry wine
                                he comes
yes he comes galloping
        on all four wheels



but does he grasp her
but does he grasp her

                shoulder,
                right,

                not a chance, they stayed
                nor would he stand

## Hard balcony on the pleasure continuum

falls off the fallen off

with a slightly bounding architecture

gives way to a pleased to be loneliness

fallen neck, out

between given off by difference to difference

a truce between
here and there

pleased to be trailing a length of red

light jumpiness of tongue

it's getting to be yes
it's getting

## Arms up and strong on the balcony

Song, as does heat, rises and people down there, speaking. Where their tongues slip or rest or stop. Willingness to climb to the heat of things means: as feet land in the crook of balcony flooring, the kindn'ss of you — is all along seeking. Perpendicular to the torso of the building, I crawl into the nearness of your elbow, angle rounding, rounding to the coil.

## Anatomy as balcony

He puts his tongue out and I rest my world on it, or
sometimes only arrival.

Either elbow suffices, a high-speed chase and these
byskaters in the way, ice or road.

Rain trying to accrue on her eyelashes.

He denies it is beer, but we children all know where to
rest our heads in times of cold.

Look left. Look right. Look to the leftest and a perimeter
around the shoulder.

A knee under construction.

She sunflowers her chest to the spring.

Hand: only when out a certain way, and holding certain.

Fingernails. The understate. Reverse. To put the world in
one of them.

## Phone call from the balcony

comes in on the thick line between there and herein. Do
you see me waving. On the other line, static and several
hundred years. Or, string two cans. We lean over the
edge in order to put an end to unsuspecting calls, but
unfortunately I heard your voice and got on the hook.
Reeling from the mad rush to respond, everyone continues
to lean and shout — around and over the periphery,
causing me to lose my breathing and my intent. I pick up
the other line, but the multiple answer is always _____ .

## External conflict inside or outside the balcony

Given no choice, as a member of the home audit.

Door #1, opens in.

Door #2

Nine thousand Roman soldiers.

# Door #3

Having been married:

on the balcony without reception on the balcony without shade on the balcony a step up the balcony a step out the balcony the balcony of old the timeless balcony the ceremonial balcony the flowers tossed from the balcony the glasses dropped from the balcony the equal opportunity balcony the brawl beneath the balcony the eyes on the balcony the grass stains near the balcony the balconic balcony the balconian balcony the balconesque balcony the poeticized balcony the fully committed balcony weathering this storm then that or the well-lit balcony the balcony in sun, sun the balcony balcony because there are two of us the same balcony but why not the luxury of two words on the balcony two suns on the balcony two children thinking ahead on the balcony right now the late afternoon sun on the balcony is enough right now I don't even have oh I can't get there via the balcony the place as the balcony takes me to the way to the balcony the way to your balcony the way to our balcony from your balcony via my balcony throwing unsmoked cigarettes from our balcony fertilizing plants from our balcony getting used to saying our our balcony our our our balcony in case one gets lost in case I get pregnant on our balcony on the the balcony in case the balcony is male, the, in case the balcony is female, the, in case it is both the balcony, that which is ours, that which we live with that we eat on that we sing from that I write of that you think of when you can't find me because I am at another balcony at an older balcony at a past balcony at a foreign balcony finally at a dark balcony which often is the case, as was the case with our first balcony on the tenth floor, the balcony from where we watched the orange lights light the campus in that horrid orange way as only orange light can, that balcony where we waited out my first dryer cycle and the balcony where we waited no we didn't wait my second dryer cycle because I put my coins in the wrong machine but in all good faith the balcony of that night is sometimes like any other balcony because it was my first loved balcony and it will be the best remembered balcony and hence the beginning or end of this balcony and why not or why, as much as one might live in or on a balcony, it's just as well, or

*Partial bridge between*

# New border collapsing

capped and sizing it prenaming it detouring it wondering
if it will do it streamed and lining it blocking the off of
it shining it on it or through it going with it to the end,
have it having given it having likened it having depicted
it having gotten used to it using it having used it the use
of it factoring in the using of it the last of it. sealed and
forgotten it. followed it to the end of it at the heart of it.
at the head of it the start of it the end of the start of it the
end of the mid of it the end of the ending of the last closed
and firm end of it to end it. and end it. the continuing
end of it. the newness of each ending for it and to it and
with it. the result of it or the less of it the non-effective
go of it. the life of it. not. the life on it. not. the life near
it. affirming it confirming it adjusting it. presuming it
and to be it or to resist it. time and it again. relationship
between preceding consuming it. time and it again and
it. the go of it. the last word of it. the heavy it. the mal-
adjusted it and might as well be it. but it is not it. the
capped and city of it. in open air it. unabashed it. should
have perhaps taken it in. the how of it, comes haunting
forth and it. concluding with it. blending it in yes. as a
new color yes. the turn of it. the left of it and I can't
stand here any more holding and holding it its tenuous
and overspeeding crumble of it mass of it the volume of
it louder than my arms can handle it can't handle it not
much longer unless it

# 2.

# CLUTCH

*hockey love letters*

this just in     accordance to the rules of)  want
                the zone

                were it to accommodate as
                much refusal as possible
                before the beginning

                on a manner of
                heat-ache
                (if you must

                                    the breeze
                                    of each
                            avid intention

# Long distance hockey

A run to the end & I waver on one foot & as if the
pond doesn't come between let's say ocean & I would
pick up some man on the street as an alter & fall into
a bench & oh the wrong bench & again & have noth-
ing to lace & I have nothing to lace or race & no
puck in the way underfoot or perfect perfect & just
ahead & on a bus & center-bound with no head up
& catch a pickup & I pass by & on the bus & noth-
ing more I can really do not much left & dance in-
stead & sleep instead & no this doesn't work & cut
& turn & left shoulder & break & yet it's never quite
& phone & doesn't work as it does with other lack
& mimosa & drinking mimosa thinking about playing
& no other kind of playing but & water too watery
but & it's summer it's summer but & I still can't &
I still can't & I still can't let it go & the glide of it
& the speed of it & no man is worth very & no sen-
tence worth completing & I want ice & I want ice &
I want & I want & I would very much like a large
sheet of ice & right about now & a hankering & a
girl with a hankering & she gets on the phone & calls
for an ice rink & the number but the number was for
pizza & she never made the right call & neither does
& neither does & neither does any ref if you are
watching the game & who's got game & who's got
game & who's got game here my kind & my time &
who & where of it & how to get to the where of it
& missing it & missing it & really nothing more I can
really do but miss it & miss it & keep an eye on
the left wing for it & a flying puck, in my sweet-
est of dreams, lachrymosa, a lift, a give, a go to and
break and away and what is this city this city is good
for this city good for and good for and good for and
food for everything but everything but everything but
& the good stuff & the faster & the wind of it, bring
it in & ship me out & back to the ice whose hand I
hold & hold & hold.

[

      if short or quick to draw
back at the top of
          [    ]
shorter breath — locality

       all dropped g[  ]loves
   whole fleet of such [ moment
   [whistle]

     cross                           ]

## Personal balcony

Let me put it this way:


You
are some sort of high-traffic balcony. Let's see: con-
structed in the fantasy-echo period or the 20th, clean
European colors a bit tousled. What narrow space —
no BBQ room, much less a party, although family and
kids are still under consideration by the higher statues.
One thing's for sure: second story:

I
am at a hockey game. I don't recall the team name, I am
too busy cheering for the forces of time or memory, here
upon this player, here upon that play, here upon the beer
in my lap. Suddenly, the puck is loose. I run out to chase
it, forgetting that you are too crowded right now, and
the play is breaking my speed          too late

[

intimations at the nearest blade
[       ]
curve — rescind — extenuate — [          ]or wrap
   aroundings at the fastdoor,
         to the[   ]quick
eyes spin to the play — circomfiting
this here,    or andlessness                                ]
      speeden'd weight continues,
                              [whistle]


                              holding     ]

36

## Zamboni-ing the balcony

resists.
ma-gritte-like,
in ma-obesity
keeps the zambona
spinning her wheels
against this ledge,
that wall, this
      point,
      line,
      break,    and
while in each coined corner
rises four ma-gretz-key
statues of dusty ice looking over the years below.

[

inclose
waiting for your

        tend, right, pinched diagonal]
long hand to left neck
     an approach[ ]ing split
screen, hat, an order to pull
to cut to deke to lift to shelf to
         [whistle]

        hook    ]

## Hockey on the 20 m² balcony

Not unlike
kissing
on a crowded train
you
then you

[

might do without — yet test
        instigation to correlation
[   ] altercate minute
          degloved vs fragility
enter who — on the board
     join or immensify, leaving it up to
         [with] [whistle]



              is conduct ]

## *We played a game of*

hockey today on the floor and as I picked myself up for the first time this year, it struck me that. Oh, pain is relative when your uncle the ref is involved, but not when there are ex's, lost ones, floating pucks and other bruises in assorted colors at stake. I didn't sub out the whole game through because I was afraid I would never find my way back in. I finally confessed of my fear of staunch, and it did me little good. I expected it would at least get me back in the game. Now I hang from the monitor up above, broadcasting the game I can't see very well from here.

[

[whistle]
what the call — for[ ]ing
                unanswered pass
lane opens inwards
        anusual, rolls new
              the we ]side
shifting loose or was this gifted —
        fine [ ]play
     to get off
        [ ] [ ] and run it out

                        ]

# Units

Distance of the heat between now (here) and hockey (yesterday at the park), as measurable in units of body heat or lack thereof. The temperatures vary, as does the distance in relation of each body that has taken any short sliver of space between here (now) and yesterday (around the time that hockey would have happened). Temperatures include: cousins of various degree and extension, parents of geographical approach, siblings, loves, unmoored others, and complete strangers. Some very close bodies arrive only in the form of some very few words, while other very strange bodies arrive in physically intrusive proportions. And where is the hockey in that.

Later, several train rides.
Still later, a dance performance.
Malleable shifting proximities between very familiar and unfamiliar bodies, new, new, old. Very old, very close, close call. Bodies carry heat together, at times in the form of love, at times in the form of very short-lived love, or new. Distance of time between bodies when moving, when not moving, when moving a small portion of surrounding air. When enough air is moved, that is enough to call it hockey, and when enough of the air has cooled, the game is long since over.

# Ice event: for 14 performers and 1 audience member

The Vehicle: a large, hollow hockey puck with the top open; about three feet in diameter, two feet high.

The Audience Member: must be small enough to fit in the Vehicle only slightly uncomfortably, perfectly upright with all limbs inside the Vehicle. Only the head should stick out. The Audience Member, once installed in the Vehicle, shall be referred to as IT.

The Cast: two full hockey teams and two referees. One of the team members is a Person of Motherly Concern in disguise; this character will try in vain to protect IT from harm.

::::::

The Cast will play a hockey game on the ice rink with IT as the puck. The game will begin in the center of the rink when the Perverted Referee stops kissing IT.

Rules are similar to hockey, plus the addition of one: no player may touch another. Any two players who touch each other even slightly must be immediately removed from the game with no replacement.

The role of IT is to verbally manipulate the players into touching each other until there are no more players left and IT can be relieved of IT's misery.

In the middle of the game is an Intermission: Two Zambonis come out, decorated as for a high school Homecoming float. The theme is Favorite Fast Food Groups: One is Hamburgers and has people in assorted Big Mac, Whopper, and Famous Star costumes. They gesticulate wildly and sometimes take a bite out of each other. The other is Tacos and has characters dressed as

Taco Bell items, Rubio's fish tacos, and Roberto's tacos who are quite groggy because they haven't slept in 24 hours.

All players speak in grunts, except for the Person of Motherly Concern who speaks gently with compassion.

If IT's vehicle tips over and IT spills out, the goalie must quickly scramble off the rink. The referees blow the whistle, then set IT upright again. The goalie may return through the gate. This all takes place in the fastest, most inefficient manner.

Sometimes the players slip and fall. This should be visually elaborate but always wordless.

Facial expressions on the players should be generally that of intimidating anger, again with the exception of the Person of Motherly Concern.

IT is allowed to do anything IT wants, as long as all limbs stay inside the vehicle.

If, or when IT cries, the game is over.

# 3.

# CRIME TO BE QUICK

Once more, she asks me,
Will you give me a kiss.
Once more, for the road,
But it's my love she must miss.

Just one I will give thee
to settle your hunger,
But after that, dear,
You will let go my finger.

## Language barrier

Men in America have a dog. I come back from Europe and you have a dog but not. Men in Europe have. I bark up the stairs and tap the tree for advice. Who has a dog. Men with dogs more likely or less fetching or slightly scarce as men without. When walking the dog, is all about the stride. I can close my eyes and walk for a long time without stepping on any dogshit. I must be in America, so I open my eyes to watch out for men instead. If I have ancient dogcrap on my shoe, I am in France and have been. The men watch, and the women have dogs. From the tree no one is shitting but is conducive to watching. I am not concerned about birds because they do not live on the ground and they barely have feet. I am concerned with the placement of my step after stepping down into soft or hard and your voice is dry. A shy dry or a bored dry or a fake, dry but really shy voice is not talking to me, thus the dog. No dog speaks in this poem, nor do I have a dog, nor am I speaking. Yet American men with dogs have. Although there may still be some French dogpoo on my shoe, I go over and talk. Talking to a dog is acceptable in any language, thus the men. After that, it is not my problem and you understand it as. You are American or European. One dog gets drunk and this is a college town. One dog has sex with a non-dog and this is pornography. One dog shoots some shit and this is a Western. I go for a walk and this is still in English and I am not interested in dogs but men.

# Tramp

And the first thing to minding is always the cold and the damper. The cold and dampid of last week's sweat. The cold and damped first-time dumpee and the cold damprue, cruel rowing in morning fog the cold dampent edge of lonely car parked overnight ad hoc the cold dam neath the fingernails, or all todamper in the morning, a break, a too-slick pause, repercussiveness. The cold of a second shot at — the dead amp of a well let's just burn —

## Dreaming about talking too soon

Making somebody's way to the light I use a borrowed voice, not yours I don't recognize it, make a few false starts, then launch.

Waiting for the right sometime to wake up, only to awaken to a spider here, spider there. Go back.

You arrive for real, this time to say that you will be there shortly, as I inversely go long, here and there a nap, a bed, a field of estrangement or flowers.

Mouth full of estrangement and flowers.

None of the flowers were edible, as it turns out. Fortunately or not my mouth is still full of the borrowed voice.

A borrowed fullness.

In the field, a mass, a gaggle of strangers.

I feel a thickness in my throat and I am forced to borrow a hand, an arm, a limb. Send the rented limb down in, to the thickness of my throat in the hopes of removing any such unwanted spiders.

None of the flowers were spiders, but the inverse was possible in a certain rented light.

A slant.

I consider making a motion, but fall prey more easily to the hiatus between each inclination. They arrive in slow succession.

As if my skin were not my own when you pull at it. I see you pulling at it and don't feel that special something. Spiders, on the other hand, I feel with an unusual or enormous weight.

Or a slant.

Call the glimmer on its act.

A woman who talks out of the side of her mind. She turns lightly in some kind of bare acknowledgement, but we all know better than to encourage her.

Lately she makes all her returns under a conditional light, very very early in the morning.

Everyone still sleeping.

She beats them all to the push, tramples lightly upon some freshly lent surface,

Everyone enough to call it everyone

She takes her shoes off, turns them in

Returns all her clothing

Shrugs off the last spider

In not an attempt but a real act of acknowledgement, a sincere pull of skin, a moist and tender slice of chicken

Yes chicken

As would fit kindly inside her mouth

Open from the first last place

Open for the long

Open for a time, a rest, a nap

A whole rest

A whole afternoon spent chewing

A whole evening spent swallowing this truth or somesuch fact

          Events declaring themselves as facts

All of it, eating a whole chicken

               Or events, all of it

                 Swallowing

And then and then

          To enter a room or make room

           In a mouth or to mouth

And then and then

        To put a mouth on the world, gently

         Easy now, before she wakes

## Force

crime to be quick

to be capable

to fall, bend, break at the cost of loyalty which loy-
alty, capacity of price

crime to be passing

by, through, under which bridge did everything get
buried, everything as in some lofty hopeful rosebush dream for some

inarticulate

unwielded

close future, hour

woman with hair like a breeze picks it up a key or
two, future children in tow, gown and arms all flapping in the wind
behind her

wind behind her hums off-key and she steps into her-
self slowly, ginger, molasses, matronly with a southerly wind

crime to be soft, to go long, to take a reach, crime to
be lengthy or claim a distance in the first place

once, under which bridge did all the water

or under which rush or gentle speed of some bridge
of any suspension

at the second place

crime to be witnessed

twice, crime to have wit
crime to be with

to be loaded, with gun, under hum and sincerity,
all of it out, all of it passing

to be loading, mild, and running

crime to wake up, miss lunch, just for a day if this
is the last occasion

running to let go

of a sandwich, lost loveliness, lifts her eyes to the
break, and beneath her faded gown

opening everything as if the realization of day,

daylight hanging bare

parts of her body which escape, which occasion

meanwhile the mob

swift, then lingering mob
lying still

crime to be had

widening mob

and to be true, meanwhile a tree, string,

parts of her body which tie in

hang on, a lack of resistance

every instance in the first place
any instance

a lost ending presents itself, gaping inflection all
dolled up for whomever, one last *take that*, or for which road on
which manipulation of bridge

a simulation of bridge

escaping mob, gone candidly
or feigned

nothing,
regrets over which lunch

## An ant against time

*The medium-term goal:*
Rush a length of words
Which continue:
       long after,
       soon again.

Its beauty
       shall be metered       as it flickers
just above a scale of

Point A to Point B
       at many, many miles per hour after hour after.


And when I inevitably encounter again a watch or a clock,
I know not only that I have been,
but may regret knowing.

## Hot wedding rods

Here, the flowers. This is a heat. They crumpled hand in hand. Compressed. Heat furthers. A couple professed it up. A hot time to. Step on it. What compelled you to tie it up. The knot. This is not. To know him is to think you know him. He is not. Or is he. Here, an army of flowers.

Two people, their boiling points. The heat that wasn't. This is a wave. An epidemic. Suited up surfers see it from afar. The horses are frightened. They get into their cars. Full of boxes. Full of coffee makers. Tea-making appliances. Ketchup-making appliances. A hamburger mold. No hamburger mold. This is a meet. Bells. A mouth, full of boxes. Full of checkmarks. Fifty miles an hour with one rear door open. Sixty miles an hour with one leg out. Seventy miles, a tongue. Panting. Reeling the curve. This is a heat. Someone in front steps on it. The horses stop in their tracks.

## Everybody's breaking point

One fine summer day, a man goes to the market, but alas having no tradable currency which he can claim as his own, fails to make a single purchase. The man is quite sure, though, as he slides open and crawls through the window of a wealthy, well-educated neighbor, that his own good and upstanding background will prevent him from committing any wrongdoing, even in such dire circumstances. After scrambling over the papers atop the desk beside the window, he walks straight to the nearest bookshelf and chooses a heavy tome about the *Méduse* shipwreck, then closes the front door quietly on his way out.

He goes home and reads. He considers returning the book, but after a certain time has passed, grows unable to see it as anyone else's but his own. He needs more books. Finding a residential neighborhood adjacent to a university, he feigns a casual stroll, carefully determines which house to enter, then goes in to take another book. He goes home and reads. He repeats this process, gradually picking up the pace, soon spending more time acquiring rather than reading books, until he has amassed more books than his home can feasibly handle. He stops inviting anyone to his home, for lack of a place for guests to sit or stand. The floorboards sag with an uneven distribution of weight, but the man is not the type to notice. One day he gives up. Carrying as many books as will fit between his two thin arms, he goes to the meeting.

::::::::

A young girl drops out of second grade out of her love of flowers. We warned her mother about this. The child's will is fierce and unreasonable, asserted through the dangerously adorable sparks in her eyes, round and young. She collects flowers incessantly and indiscriminately:

from the sidewalk, from before-hours flower shops, from the bouquet of roses clutched between the fingers of a young man in love. She sneaks into weddings an hour before they commence and plucks a single stem out of each bouquet adorning the aisles. This is the ritual of her every day, and well before four in the afternoon, she has usually gathered more flowers than she can carry between her small arms. It was not her intention to attend the meeting, as she was only looking for more flowers, but it's just as well.

::::::

A young drinker, having spent all his money on video games, baseball cards, and a somewhat rare dragonfly collection, wanders casually through the bar. Loitering around tables where people have their backs to him, he sneaks a small sip out of every beverage glass within reach. After every sip, he returns the glass to exactly the same location, so that the owner of the drink senses nothing out of the ordinary, while being forced to tip the head back one or two degrees extra in order to get to the drink. Many people do in fact notice this, but at such a mild and non-threatening level that the thought is dismissed in no time at all. The young drinker hops bars this way, never visiting the same bar twice. He collects their business cards in order to remember where not to return. After years in the same megalopolis, he moves on to the next, not because he has exhausted all the bars, but out of a desire to overhear fragments of conversation in a new or different language, in order to understand less, feel less comfortable. This new megalopolis is where he finds himself at the meeting. He is drunk. At the meeting he continues to sip from other people's drinks, but strangely, they all seem to notice, and even nudge their glasses slightly in his direction.

::::::

The meeting takes place by a lake. There is a man who has been there since the very beginning of it all. As people arrive, lugging with them more whatevers than they really are able to handle, he sits them down without a word and relieves them of their books, their flowers, their alcohol. He dives into the bottom of the lake and plants these objects there one by one, respectfully, in a neat and orderly fashion, as if planting a row of corn at the bottom of the odd-figured lake. The man does not read books, or collect flowers, or sip alcohol, but is working on gaining a little bit, just a little bit more every single day, of capacity in his lungs. One day he will run the Boston marathon in one single breath, and all of us who have ever been to that lake will thank him for it and cheer him on, throwing our books and flowers and booze at him as he whizzes by oh-so-very quickly.

## Group

Not dark, nor an intersection, yet one is compelled towards a headlight in the open throughness of day: naked insistent arrival at a limited line. Original intentions never materialized, and all we are left with is a wake, an immeasurable pain quotient, and the peaceful dreams of the street singer. One new patient puts in a request for "Georgia," and everyone sits down in a fit of nostalgia, though no one has ever been and the majority are unsure of which country. The good news is that suddenly there is an everyone, as well as an old sweet intersection. Arms abound, but as darkness descends we are instructed, in 7.5 languages and two dialects of body language, to together hold our hands up to hold it, hold it back.

# Glass

In pursuit of red dress, she walked into the bathroom, and tried to pee standing up. She noticed the angle her legs made, and in so doing dropped her calculator in the tub. She then stood one leg deep, gathered the other leg faithfully and inserted it into a new pant leg. From the next leg she peeled off last year's inertia and tripped, clamored upstairs to her bedroom frame where she spread, distinct, and shouted pretty sale prices through no glass of her own.

## The music's seeping through

your glass, she reports. She sings to me enough as it is. She begins to open her eyes in protest, but instead follows the music right out of the glass, and out of my hand.

*Every day it strays a little*

this line called intent, first thing in my every morning. Loosening into the day in a passive mission called this is it, line after my own heat. A loose pile of it, said heat. You slip back towards sleep and I suspect my values as they reach for some kind of standard issue contour, which I have never seen. Your sleep indicates that there is nothing out of the ordinary, and I continue to turn in place, shaking little pebbles off as I make my rounds. When I've lifted the final stone and heaved it over the edge, a man wakes up on the other side of town feeling a heavy pit in his stomach. His connection to you is yet to be declared, but the distance between both of your bodies is just at the limit of how far I am willing to travel for the sake of a kiss. Hurry up, I tell you. You roll over.

# Crossings

to stand still and take it, to hold my hands, nay arms, all the way out until it doesn't hurt anymore, to close up the breaks in my voice, as if I could, what would I. If I stand still like so in the middle of the intersection, a voice on one end would be reminded of the village idiot, while a neighboring voice would feel a familiar sympathy, while yet another would stare, a small child that would stare at me in its graceless wonder and what would it, what could it know. And what would I know as they unleashed the people on me, heretofore held back by cages, leashes, traffic lights, or conscience, what would I know as they stormed their purposeful gaits past me, through me, over, and under my arms, my very arms I still hold out as if in vanity or hope, and carrying what else but the swirl of passing people as they pass by me, through, over, under, and beyond it all and I stand still and take it.

## Attendance

The man who seems to be dressed very nicely. The woman who guffawed and small flecks of food flew out of her mouth. The woman who brought her child. The woman who walks very, yes very elegantly in her heels. The man in tuxedo. The women wearing the same color dress and shoes. The man bringing food to people's tables. The other man bringing food. The man going around with bottles of wine. The woman who has been sitting next to me for seven minutes now. The woman across the table with a rash on the side of her neck and many many very thin very fine bracelets on her left my right arm. The woman taking photographs with a very large camera and a very large flash. The man and woman smiling in front of the camera. The man smiling next to him, whether or not he is in the photograph. The man smiling in the other direction, his back in the photograph. The woman smiling at that man, her elbow possibly in the photograph. The woman now sitting next to me and eating very steadily. The magenta jacket hanging on the back of the chair on the other side of me. The man whispering something devilishly to another man in the front of the room, holding an instrument made of metal. The man who seems to dance while standing still. The woman holding his hand, who seems to stand still while dancing. The man who tripped on a cord, then immediately recovered, but looked nervously all around to see if anyone saw him. The man holding two

women's hands at the same time in the same
hand, with a wine glass in the other hand.
The women towards whom they are headed.
The man with a very wide arm span. The
woman hitting her fork against her glass. The
man hitting his fork against his glass.
The man hitting his glass. The other man.
The other woman. The other people hitting.
The last people to keep hitting. The woman
who kisses the man. The other woman who
kisses the other man. The woman who
kisses two men. The man who drinks his
glass down in fourteen seconds. The man
who drinks another in eighteen seconds.
The woman with a smudge of lipstick on her
teeth. The man speaking enthusiastically
into a microphone, smiling and making
many people laugh. The man who seems
to have a twinkle in his eye. The woman who
seems to be delighted. The man who has been
speaking now for quite a long time.
The woman sniffling into her napkin. The
man who seems to encourage the woman.
The men and women who applaud.The people
who start playing their metal instruments.
The man and woman dancing slowly. The
man dancing with no discernable speed.
The woman dancing who ate very quickly in
the seat next to me. The woman spinning
her dress as she dances. The woman who
dances with first one man then another then
another. The man who seems to know the
words to the song. The man who seems to
be singing. The woman who walks around
slowly letting people kiss her cheek.

## With a gun under her knuckle, she

untied her seatbelt from the floor, peeled herself away from the fireplace, and rested her eyes on the dessert tray.

# Hurry home honey

### 1.
On a warm November Sunday in the middle of a suburban morning, an angry man takes leave of his constipated woman, just as she is having a longish bout with her bowels while reading about the shipwreck of the *Admiral Graf Spee* and wondering vaguely if there are really people out there who enjoy the smell of their own excrement. He leaves no note, takes nothing with him, and locks the door behind him as he leaves, slipping the keys into his usual left pocket.

### 2.
A few weeks later, the lack of indication that her man may be returning compels the woman to start calling around, to find out if he is dead. She searches all the neighborhood tombstones for his name, flowers in hand, just in case. She then asks at all the local gasoline stands, then the Wal-Mart, the barbershop around the corner, and finally, his favorite bar. Coming up with very little information, she then goes looking for all the regional hit men to see if they know anything, then all the gangs, then the mailman, then the ladies on the stoop. Nothing, almost nothing.

### 3.
In the garage of her own home, she digs up a photo of her missing man, and sends it, along with a modest handling fee, to the NCMEP (National Center for Missing and Exploited Persons), to get his picture on the side of a milk carton. For a while she is filled with a sense of hope and accomplishment, but in a little over a week, the photo is returned to her with a note attached, saying that they are very sorry for her loss, but the milk-carton project has been replaced by a downloadable screen-saver program with rotating images of missing

children. They also note that they are the NCME*C*, who deals with children, and not the NCME*P*, who deals with persons. They claim that her person is too old to be treated as a child and that she should know better. After writing an angry letter to the milk-carton people demanding her money back, the woman decides to take matters into her own hands, and sits down to make a flyer.

4.
Struggling to find the appropriate words, she begins with "Missing." "Last seen." "Responds to – ." Height. Eye color. Reward. Honks when blowing nose. Large bottom lip. Then she runs out of descriptive phrases. She simply carries on, and makes copies of the brand-new flyer, featuring the photo that was returned from the milk-carton people. After posting her flyers everywhere within a five-mile radius of home, she mails the remaining copies to a friend who is good with these things, and considers her job done, at least for the time being.

5.
A few weeks later the lack of phone calls, faxes, and e-mails she has received regarding her man compels the woman to sit down and cry a two-gallon bucket of tears. Trying to practice what her mother had taught her about not being wasteful, she gets up and waters her plants, then the neighbor's plants, then the large oak tree by the sidewalk, with the contents of the bucket. Having thus purged some, but not all, of her pain, she then goes back inside, sits down again at the work table in the garage, and writes a novel, titling it *Hurry Home Honey.*

6.
In spite of the unfashionable choice of title, the book becomes a bestseller and large bookstore chains all over the United States and Canada stock not only the book, but a cleverly designed T-shirt bearing its title, and

display them both prominently in the entryway during the month of December.


7.

A tourist on vacation in Buttonwillow, California buys both the book and shirt, returns to Belgium, his home and native land, and after getting teased by his stupid illiterate friends about the shirt, decides to only wear it when he goes to the gym.


8.

A man reads the writing on the shirt, and looks at his watch.

## Biographical Note:

Sawako Nakayasu was born in Japan and has lived mostly in the US since the age of six.

She is the author of *So we have been given time  Or* (Verse Press, 2004), *Nothing fictional but the accuracy or arrangement (she* (Quale Press, 2005), and *Texture Notes* (forthcoming from Letter Machine, 2009).

Books of translations include *Four from Japan* (Litmus Press / Belladonna Books, 2006), *To the Vast Blooming Sky* by Chika Sagawa (Seeing Eye Books, 2007), and *For the Fighting Spirit of the Walnut* by Takashi Hiraide (New Directions, 2008).

Her own poetry has been translated into Japanese, Swedish, Arabic, Chinese, and Vietnamese.

She is also the editor of *factorial*, an annual of collaboration and translation. She holds an MFA from Brown University and has received grants from the NEA and PEN for translating Japanese poetry.

This book was designed and computer typeset by Rosmarie Waldrop in 10 pt. Palatino, with Handwriting-Dakota half-titles. Cover by Keith Waldrop. Printed on 55 lb. Writers' Natural (an acid-free paper), smyth-sewn and glued into paper covers by McNaughton & Gunn in Saline, Michigan. There are 1000 copies.